LEFT-HANDED SEWING

LEFT-
HANDED
SEWING

SALLY COWAN

Drawings by Kurt Loftus

VNR VAN NOSTRAND REINHOLD COMPANY
NEW YORK CINCINNATI TORONTO LONDON MELBOURNE

To my grandmother, Kerr, who shared with me her love
for sewing the "left" way, and to my husband, who is forever
encouraging me.

Printed in the United States of America

Designed by Diane Saxe

Published by Van Nostrand Reinhold Company Inc.
135 West 50th Street
New York, New York 10020

Van Nostrand Reinhold Company Limited
Molly Millars Lane
Wokingham, Berkshire RG11 2PY, England

Van Nostrand Reinhold
480 La Trobe Street
Melbourne, Victoria 3000, Australia

Macmillan of Canada
Division of Gage Publishing Limited
164 Commander Boulevard
Agincourt, Ontario M1S 3C7, Canada

16   15   14   13   12   11   10   9   8   7   6   5   4   3   2   1

Library of Congress Cataloging in Publication Data

Cowan, Sally.
    Left-handed sewing.

    Includes index.
    1. Sewing. I. Title.
TT715.C68   1984   646.2′042′024081   83–16706
ISBN 0-442-20933-9 (pbk.)

CONTENTS

6 *Contents*

PREFACE

Among the definitions of "left-handed" in *Webster's International Dictionary* are "clumsy, awkward, insincere or dubious." Well, to the large numbers of us lefties—15 percent of the population, according to government figures—these unkind words come as no surprise. It is easy to be clumsy or awkward when you are bumping elbows at the dinner table, wrestling with wrong-sided pay phones and vending machines, or trying to restring a guitar in reverse! And good-natured as we may be, our outlook may become a little strained, even insincere or dubious, when too much of our lives is wasted translating a right-handed world into left-handed terms.

Luckily most of these adjustments are made while we are young. But today, as more and more people are discovering the pleasures of handcrafts and home workshops, we left-handed folk are once again straining to adjust to right-handed diagrams, tools, and instructional materials.

This is particularly true in home sewing. In these days, when a growing number of people are conscious of fashion and quality and fewer of us can afford fine clothes, the lure of home sewing is undeniable. The cost differential on one season's wardrobe, between readymade and homemade, would buy a good sewing machine. And after thirty-six years of sewing for myself and others, I am still amazed at the ingenuity of the pattern companies in producing more beautiful and more explicit patterns every season.

There is just one little catch. Virtually the entire home-sewing industry is designed and marketed for the right-handed sewer. When you consider the thousands and thousands of lefties busily turning sewing directions around in our heads, it is a wonder that there are not more left-handed diagrams and materials. At present, the only solution is to hold confusing patterns or diagrams to a mirror while sewing.

After decades of wrestling with right-handed instructions and diagrams, I am delighted to write a reference book for myself and other left-handed sewers. At last, sewing approached from the left, and, as we all know, left is best! A word of warning to my readers: cast aside the urge to reverse directions. Remember that these stitches are done your way, the "left" way.

BASIC TOOLS FOR HAND SEWING

ALTHOUGH SEWING MACHINES have become highly sophisticated, handwork is still necessary when stitching a hem, basting a seam, finishing a buttonhole, tailoring a jacket, sewing on trim and buttons. Most of these little jobs have been a necessary part of sewing since we traded in animal skins for cloth. And in this age of answering machines and computers that do everything but walk the dog, the basic tools of hand stitching have barely changed from those early days.

But the basic tools have been developed and improved. In a few cases, there are even special tools for the left-handed sewer. In the next pages we will discuss the correct tools for each job and where you can find those precious left-handed scissors.

Before you can make use of the information in this book you must familiarize yourself with the Fabric Key, which allows you to see what part of the fabric is being sewn.

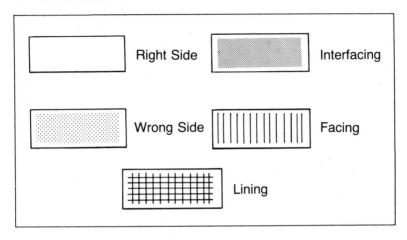

SCISSORS

At the sewing machine or when hand stitching, scissors and shears play an important part. They do many jobs from the first cutting of the pattern and fabric to the final trimming of stray threads. Sewing scissors (3- to 6-inch blades) and shears (blades longer than 6 inches) are *not* for working in the kitchen, cutting flowers or paper, or trimming nails. These tasks blunt the blades, and for sewing you need sharp, well-maintained instruments that will cut your fabric flat and clip without pulling or—heaven forbid—missing the mark.

For the left-handed person to make do with right-handed scissors is both irritating and physically harming. (I began to sew years before left-handed scissors were available, and I have a heavily calloused thumb to show for it.) When selecting your scissors and shears keep in mind that there are three types:

- Left handled and right blade (left thumb controls the right blade)
- Left handled and left blade (left thumb controls the left blade)
- Right handled and right blade (right thumb controls the right blade)

Most left-handed sewers who have been struggling with right-handed scissors are most comfortable with the first type of scissors. If you are willing to retrain yourself, or if you are buying scissors for a left-handed youngster who is learning to sew, the left-handed handle and blade will turn out to be the most comfortable and efficient in the long run. If at all possible, try out your scissors before you buy them to make sure the handle and angle of the blade are comfortable for you. See the box below for addresses of two companies whose scissors I have used for years. They have a selection of left-handed blades for most sewing needs.

When selecting scissors and shears, look for clean plating, a uniform width and angle of cutting edge, and an adjustable screw. If the blades resist opening and closing, choose a different pair. Be sure to oil the screw occasionally and then wipe clean.

Once you have your scissors in hand, use them with caution and respect. Once scissors have been put to cloth, the action is done. You cannot glue the pieces back together. Cut only when you are fresh, alert, and least likely to be distracted. The lower blade should slide along the table without lifting the fabric (Fig. 1–1). Pinking shears or scalloping shears are not for cutting out a pattern; use these only for finishing seams. You should never turn fabric while cutting; place the layout so that you are in a comfortable position for reaching and cutting. Start cutting at one end of the fabric while the other end is supported or rolled up. Use long strokes for the straight edges and short strokes for the curved edges. Cut pattern notches outward. When clipping or slashing use the point of the scissors.

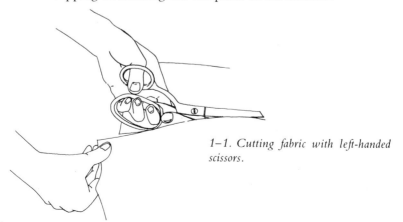

1–1. Cutting fabric with left-handed scissors.

Scissors Directory

Wiss

> The Cooper Group
> 3535 Glenwood Avenue
> P.O. Box 30100
> Raleigh, NC 27622
> Phone: (919) 781-7200

Available left-hand scissors:

- 3778T Contura-lite 8 inch shears: nickel-plated blades; comfortable contoured steel reinforced handle; simulated tortoiseshell color
- 427½LH solid steel 7½ inch dressmaker: hot drop-forged nickel-plated black handles
- CB-7LH solid steel 7½ inch Pinker-Wiss pinking shears: hot drop-forged with standard teeth, nickel-plated blades; black handles
- 20LH solid steel 10 inch professional: hot drop-forged nickel-plated blades; black handles

Marks

> Marks International, Inc.
> 60 Wells Avenue
> Newton, MA 02159
> Phone: (617) 965-4000

Available left-hand scissors:

- Serra Sharp (404-8 inch) dressmaker shears
- Knife edge (406-8 inch) dressmaker shears
- Enameled handle (407BLH) pinking shears, 7½ inches
- Knife edge (771-8 inch) lightweight dressmaker shears

PINS

Pins do not distinguish between the right and the left hand, but there *is* a "left" way to place them (Fig. 1–2A). Notice (Fig. 1–2B) that all the heads are on the left side. When machine sewing, always pin across the seam and remove each pin before the presser foot travels over it. When pinning a pattern, place pins across a seam line to prevent unnecessary wrinkles.

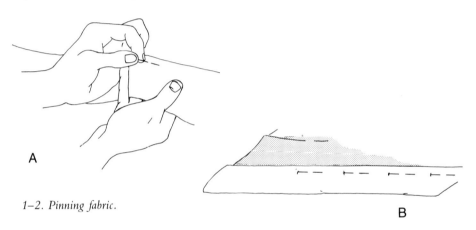

A

1–2. Pinning fabric.

B

NEEDLES AND THREAD

Naturally there is no such thing as a left-handed needle, but there is a "left" way to thread the needle. More about that later.

The most important thing is to pick the correct needle for the task at hand. As a general rule, needles for sewing are shorter than needles for needlepoint or crewel work. There are several types of sewing needles for different jobs. For each type, sizes range from a low number, indicating a coarse needle, to a high number, indicating a finer needle. I would suggest buying a package with a variety of sizes and making your choice as the need arises.

Hand needles are selected with consideration for construction of fabric, weight and type of fabric, type of thread, size and weight of thread, and intended use. For those with vision problems, there are also needles with an opening at the top so that you needn't focus on the eye of the needle to be able to thread it.

There are sixteen types of needles that are commonly used, seven of which are the most popular. When you look at the differences it is easy to see why it is so important to take time to select your needle (Fig. 1–3).

A. Ballpoint needle. This needle has a rounded tip and a small rounded eye. It slides through the fabric rather than piercing it, and is great for knits and lingerie fabrics.

B. Chenille needle. This needle has a long oval eye of extra proportion. It carries multiple strands of thread in embroidery work.

C. Curved needle. This needle is a semicircle and designed with a large oval eye. It is used in upholstery and for lampshades and mattresses.

D. Glover's needle. This needle tapers to a three-faceted point. The "wedge" shape is designed to penetrate leather and plastic without tearing or splitting.

E. Tufting needle. This is a coarse needle designed with a large, oval eye and a slightly curved, flattened, and faceted wide end tapering to a point. This pointed end penetrates cloth without tearing and splitting. It also permits passage of multiple strands of yarn or thread and is useful when weaving ribbon through the fabric.

F. Milliner's needle. This is a very thin and long needle, often used in basting or for feathering and shirring.

G. Calyx-eye needle. This needle is designed with an oval eye and a slotted opening on the side. This is often used by sight-impaired people. The thread is pulled into the eye through the slot on the edge of the eye.

In our mother's day, the only problem in selecting thread was matching the color to the fabric. But today we are faced with a

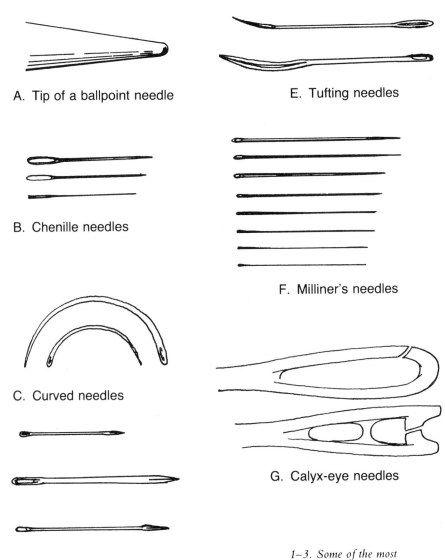

A. Tip of a ballpoint needle

E. Tufting needles

B. Chenille needles

F. Milliner's needles

C. Curved needles

G. Calyx-eye needles

D. Glover's needles

1–3. Some of the most common types of needles.

variety of threads, and we may need a little guidance through this wonderland of plastic spools.

There are so many good threads on the market today that choice is becoming a matter of what to *avoid,* because there are bad threads too. And once you have watched a seam giving way after the second washing because of weak thread, you'll never buy that brand again. To help you avoid such a disaster, here are two warnings. First, throw away all the pure cotton thread you've been hoarding for five years or more. Natural fibers, no matter how good to begin with, do deteriorate. Even mercerized cotton will weaken. (*Never* buy cotton thread unless it is mercerized; this chemical process pre-shrinks and strengthens the fibers.) Second, "bargain" spools of polyester thread may not be a good buy. I know they are hard to resist, but before you start sewing with them, test their strength by tugging a strand till it breaks. Then compare it with a more expensive brand. If you can notice a difference in strength, toss the weak one out unless you enjoy mending split seams. Cotton thread is the choice for cotton and polycotton fabrics, except knits. Polyester and cotton wrapped polyester are better for knits or stretchable sewing because of their willingness to stretch slightly under pressure. And high-quality polyester thread is good for almost anything. Buttonhole twist is a thread developed by twisting 3 strands together loosely. This thread is strong and smooth and ideal for topstitching or hand-worked buttonholes.

Many people feel that thread is "programmed" to knot on purpose. Actually there is a reason that thread doesn't always run smooth. Thread has a one-way nap. If pulled through the cloth in the

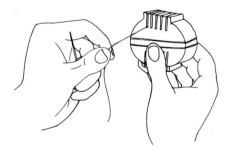

1–4. Beeswax.

direction it comes off the spool, it will not knot. Dragging the thread through beeswax (Fig. 1–4) will also help to prevent snarling. If you are sewing with a double thread, knot each thread separately. Even beyond the first stitch the thread tends to stay untangled because of the double knots.

THIMBLES

If your grandmother taught you how to use a thimble, she probably showed you the "right" way. The "left" way is simply to move it to your left hand.

Using a thimble is a personal decision, but once you have learned how to use it, it does cut down on the holes in the finger. Sizes range from 6 to 11, to fit the middle finger of your sewing hand. Use it to guide the eye-end of the needle through the fabric.

GETTING STARTED

THE FIRST STEP is often the hardest step. But after you have completed your first garment, you will be happy to start each new project.

LAYING OUT THE PATTERN

In commercial pattern instructions, the cutting layout of the pattern on fabric is set up from the right to the left. That is, the broader edges of each pattern piece tend to be at the right. The narrower ends—waistlines of skirts, shoulders of blouses and bodices—are at the left of the layout. As you might suspect, the assumption of the pattern company is that you will be pinning from the right to the left. Those of you who have been sewing for years have probably gotten used to following these diagrams. But lefties know how awkward it is.

For those of you just starting out, now is the time to learn the old mirror trick. Hold the diagram to a mirror and get a reverse image;

then pin your pattern to the fabric the "left" way. Working from the left to the right, you'll be able to pin down the broader edges of each piece first and work toward the narrow, detailed edges without trying to pin backwards. When you've gotten used to reversing the printed diagram, you will be glad you made the effort.

Here are a few tips about pinning patterns to fabric. First, work in a place where you will not have to move anything until you are finished cutting. If you enjoy the luxury of a cutting table in your sewing room, count your blessings. But if you use the dining room table or the living room floor, do wait until the kids and pets are out of the way. Once you start pinning, the fabric must stay flat until you are finished. Otherwise you may discover—after you have cut—that you have a fold or a bias pull that was never designed in the garment.

Speaking of bias, those "grain of fabric" arrows printed on virtually every pattern piece are critically important. Any deviation from the exact vertical or horizontal weave of the material creates a slight or major bias. And bias "gives." (If you are not familiar with bias, pull at the two opposite corners of a handkerchief. See how the fabric stretches. That is why bias skirts drape so beautifully. But when not called for, that same stretchiness will ruin the line of most designs.)

The next tips deal with order of pinning. It is a good idea to pin along the grain arrows first (one pin at each end of the arrow). By pinning the entire pattern down in this manner you can check the spacing and correct any mistakes with a minimum of unpinning and repinning. And there is less chance for moving the pattern off the grain during complete pinning.

After you have pinned along the grain arrows you should "anchor" each pattern piece by placing a pin at the corners. For example, you would anchor the lower corners and the points of the sleeves and bodice. Together with the pins along the grain line, these pins keep your pattern from twisting or shifting as you pin along curves.

When working with very light or slippery fabrics, you may find it handy to pin the two sides of the folded material together at points along the fold line and the selvage; this will keep it folded as you want it. If you have pre-washed a pure cotton to make sure it will not shrink after all your labor (which is highly recommended), do not forget to iron it before laying out your pattern. Remember: the best pattern design in the world will not work if you do not keep the fabric flat when you are pinning.

TAILOR TACKS

For many home sewers, the invention of tracing wheels and colored carbon paper ranks just behind the invention of the sewing machine. What a boon when it comes to reproducing all those lines and dots the pattern companies distribute over their tissue paper. Unfortunately, tracing paper has a drawback, one you already know if you have ever mistakenly marked on the right side of your fabric. These marks often resist washing out. And when carbon is used on a light-colored fabric it can show through, "shadowing" your darts or seam lines.

There *is* a solution. Tailor tacks are the time-honored way of reproducing pattern markings, and they are easier than you ever suspected.

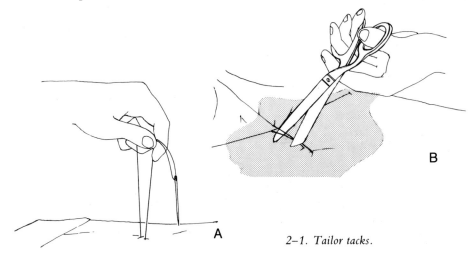

2-1. Tailor tacks.

First, thread your needle and leave the thread at least 12 inches long. No knot is needed. Use thread of contrasting color to your fabric. (This is a good time to use up leftover spools.)

With the pattern still pinned to the fabric, insert the needle down through the pattern and fabric, then back up again ½ inch—only once. Hold up the long ends of the thread (Fig. 2–1A) and cut them off long. Do each pattern marking in the same manner.

As you finish each section, unpin the pattern. Then carefully pull the tissue off the fabric and cut the threads between the two fabric pieces (Fig. 2–1B). Do this on a table, rather than in your lap. The threads will remain for the length of time you need them. When you no longer need them, just pull them out.

Once you have gotten used to making tailor tacks, you will throw out those sheets of blue, yellow, purple, and white tracing paper. Nonwashable carbon stains will never darken your darts again.

PRESSING/IRONING

Like basting and making tailor tacks, ironing as you sew may seem like a step that can just as well be skipped by the time-conscious sewer. And as with the other steps, it just isn't so. The few moments it takes to press down a seam or a dart will more than repay you in results.

There are certain areas, particularly where seams intersect with other seams, that you may never be able to iron properly after the garment is finished. These places include underarms, side pockets, trouser crotches, collars, and plackets. That first pressing helps to set the fabric and shows you that your seam was sewn properly, no puckers or bunching.

Today, after almost thirty years of wash and wear clothing, it is just possible that some readers have never picked up an iron. And for you, I have some more bad news. Lefties are again at a disadvantage because the cords of many irons are tilted the wrong way. No solutions on this one, just practice.

BASIC HAND STITCHES

LEARNING TO SEW involves mastering the basic hand stitches and knowing how and when to use them.

THREADING THE NEEDLE

Like boiling an egg, threading a needle is something we assume is simple. And it is—once you know how. Here are a few pointers.

To thread the needle, hold the needle in your right hand. With your left hand, bring the end of the thread off the spool and direct it through the eye (Fig. 3–1A). If the thread is broken or frayed, cut a clean end. If it "fans" open, wet it and twist it in the direction of the thread's twist. *After* the needle is threaded cut the thread from the spool (Fig. 3–1B). That way you remember to knot the end you've just cut; the grain of the thread is then correct, and you minimize snarling and knotting.

To knot the end, hold the needle in your right hand and grip the end of the thread between your left index finger and thumb. Wind the thread around your index finger twice (Fig. 3–1C) and, by using your thumb, roll the circle of thread off your index finger. The two circles should twist around each other. Now slide your finger down the end of the thread, encouraging the circles to condense into a compact little knot (Figs. 3–1D and 3–1E). This may take a bit of practice, but it is quick and easy once you know how to do it. If the knot comes out with a dangling loop, clip it off and try again. If you wet your fingers first, it will be much easier.

Now you are ready to sew—the "left" way.

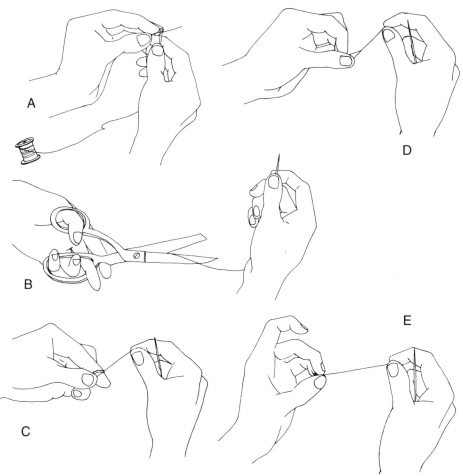

3–1. Threading the needle.

BASTING

The most basic stitch of all is the basting stitch, whether it be the uneven, even, or diagonal stitch. Basting is temporary sewing. Its most obvious use is for checking the fit of a garment. Because the big stitches are so easy to pull out and the thread ends aren't knotted, you can sew the seams quickly and try the garment on. Fitting errors can be spotted early in the sewing process and easily corrected.

Basting is also used to match stripes or plaids precisely, to apply interfacing, to hold down zippers, to apply pockets, and to stabilize hemlines before the final hemming is done.

Many pattern directions suggest that you pin before basting. Though it may sometimes seem like a bother, pinning and basting are steps that ensure a professional-looking garment. Don't overlook them.

Baste slightly *inside* the usual ⅝-inch seam allowance. Always remove your basting thread before pressing the garment.

Even Basting Use this stitch for stress areas, such as set-in sleeves, areas that require control, and seams that must be eased. ("Ease" is when the two edges of fabric being stitched together are of slightly different lengths; the longer edge is "eased" or slightly gathered to match the shorter.)

Working from left to right, take ¼-inch stitches, evenly spaced (Fig. 3–2). Gather a few stitches at a time before pulling the needle through the cloth.

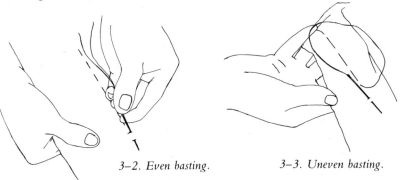

3–2. *Even basting.*   3–3. *Uneven basting.*

Uneven Basting Use this stitch for nonstress areas. Marking hems, marking center fronts or center backs, catching linings are all possible with uneven basting.

Work in a manner similar to even basting, but the ¼-inch stitches are taken 1 inch apart (Fig. 3–3).

Diagonal Basting Use this for holding linings, interfacings, and facings in place during a fitting. It looks like a padding stitch cut in half. That may be why it is called "tailor basting." On the top side the stitch is diagonal, but on the underside the stitch is short and horizontal.

The needle is placed at right angles to the turned edge of the garment. Always work from the wrong side of the garment, left to right. The stitches are taken parallel to each other with the needle pointing from left to right (Fig. 3–4); this produces a diagonal stitch on the right side.

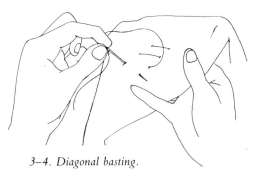

3–4. Diagonal basting.

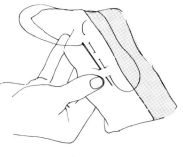

3–5. Fastening stitch.

FASTENING STITCHES

There are two stitches used by experienced sewers to begin or end a line of handstitching. Their advantage over the simple knot is that they do not strain or tug the fabric at a single concentrated point, thereby advertising on the finished product exactly where you started.

Fastening Stitch This stitch has one function—to begin a row of hand stitching. It is simple, effective, and stronger than a knot. Starting on the wrong side, pull thread through the fabric. At a point ¼ inch to the left, sew through to the other side and bring the needle back again at the point it first emerged (Fig. 3–5). Repeat this stitch two more times without pulling too tight.

Backstitch Tack This is a slightly fancier stitch that serves both to start and to end a row. It will prevent the threads from ever coming loose, and it is preferred by professionals. Start on the wrong side and bring thread through to the right side of fabric. Take a ½-inch stitch, beginning ¼ inch to the left and coming out ¼ to the right of where the thread emerged (Fig. 3–6A). Repeat the first stitch two or three times (Fig. 3–6B). To finish, take one extra stitch and the thread will be secured. Leave a ½-inch tail of thread.

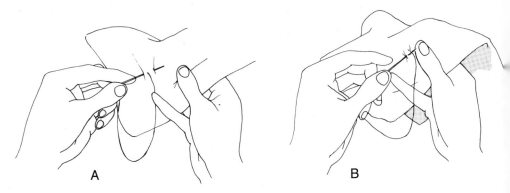

A   B

3–6. Backstitch tack.

BACKSTITCH

Before the invention of the sewing machine, the backstitch was used to hold garments together. It is the strongest of all the hand stitches and looks like machine stitching on the top. But the stitches overlap on the underside. You must take only one stitch at a time, because you have to go forward and then backward, forward and then backward. This is what reinforces the seam.

Even Backstitch This is used for making and repairing seams.

Starting on the left, bring the needle and thread to the top layer of the pieces being sewn. Insert the needle through all fabric layers ⅛ inch *behind* the point where the thread emerges (Fig. 3–7A). Bring the needle and thread out the same distance *beyond* the point at which the thread first emerged. Continue this pattern, being sure the needle and thread are one-half a stitch length behind and beyond the thread from the previous stitch (Fig. 3–7B).

Half-Backstitch This is used for repairing seams; it also holds lapels in place. It is similar to the even backstitch, but the stitches don't meet on the top layer. Starting on the left, insert the needle through all fabric layers ⅛ inch behind the point where the thread emerges, but this time bring it out twice this distance beyond that point (Fig. 3–8).

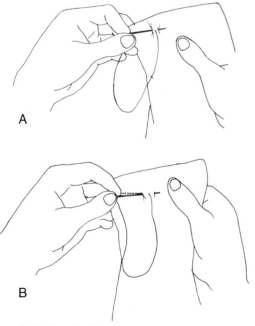

3–8. *Half backstitch.*

3–7. *Even backstitch.*

BLANKET STITCH

Use this for an edge finish, a decorative hem, or a variety of hand-finished edges. You may also use it instead of a buttonhole stitch.

Be sure to start on the right side of the fabric and work to the left. To keep the stitches even, mark a guideline with chalk or basting thread ¼ inch above seamline. Knot the thread and insert the needle from the bottom side. Bring the needle to the top side on the guideline. Hold the thread and needle ¼ inch to the left of the first stitch, inserting the needle perpendicular to the edge. Keep the thread behind the needle (Fig. 3–9) and pull the needle through the loop. The loop must be behind the needle at all times. Continue your stitches and keep them evenly spaced, not too tight. End with a backstitch tack on the underside.

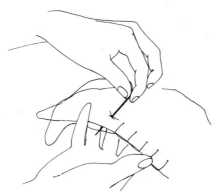

3–9. Blanket stitch.

Blanket Stitch Tack This is used for joining two fabric layers together: joining a facing to a garment. It is merely for tacking purposes.

Work from right to left and be sure the facing is folded back and the needle is pointing toward you. The thread should be fastened to the facing. These stitches are spread 1 to 2 inches apart. The needle must be vertical to the edge. Pass the needle over the thread (Fig. 3–10) and go through the interfacing and then through the facing, making sure there is slack between the stitches.

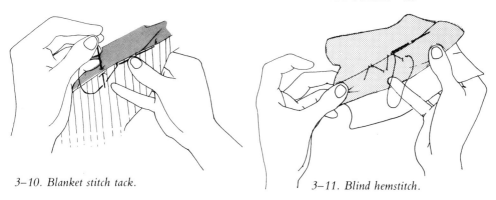

3–10. Blanket stitch tack.

3–11. Blind hemstitch.

BLIND HEMSTITCH

Use this for hemming and for holding facings in place. It is especially good when hemming heavy fabrics. It is also used to join linings and to finish waistbands and collars . It is called a blindstitch because it is invisible from the right side of the garment.

Attach a single strand of thread with a fastening stitch. Work from left to right with the needle pointing left. Place pins ¼ inch down from the edge you are about to sew. As you take horizontal stitches, hold the ¼-inch edge back with your thumb (Fig. 3–11). Catch one or two threads on the garment and, moving to the right, take your next stitch on the facing—catching a few threads at a time. Alternate stitches from garment to hem or facing to garment. Secure with a backstitch tack.

CATCH STITCH

This stitch is for holding two layers of fabric together while giving a degree of flexibility. Also holds facings in place and linings to a garment. It is sometimes used to secure pleats and tucks, but mostly for attaching raw edges of facings and interfacings to the wrong side of garment.

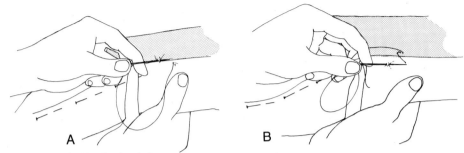

3–12. Catch stitch.

Secure thread to the top layer of fabric with a fastening stitch. Notice the direction of this stitch. You start at the right; your needle faces the right; but the stitches are moving to the left. This is what causes the thread to cross itself each time. Take a small horizontal stitch in one layer of fabric (Fig. 3–12A). Catch one or two threads only. Take another horizontal stitch near the edge of the other layer of fabric (Fig. 3–12B). The stitches form a zigzag pattern. Don't pull the stitches too tight and keep the stitches small. End with a backstitch tack.

Catch Stitch Tack Use this for holding garment sections (such as facings) to a front section. Because this is used for tacking, the stitches are at least 1 inch apart.

Work from right to left with the facing folded back. The needle should point right. Catch the thread in the facing (Fig. 3–13A) and,

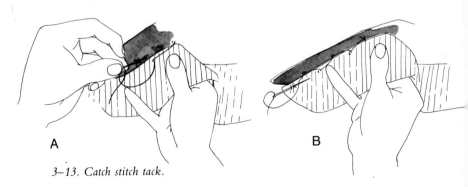

3–13. Catch stitch tack.

1 inch to the left, take a small stitch in the interfacing (Fig. 3–13B). Bring the needle and thread through. Bring needle 1 inch to the left and catch a thread in the facing. Be sure there is a slight slack between stitches.

HEMMING STITCHES

These are used to secure the hem edge to a garment.

Slant Hemming Stitch This secures hem edges to a garment; used most often when seam binding is used. These are small diagonal stitches taken ¼ inch apart.

Secure a single thread with a fastening stitch on the wrong side of the hem. Take your first stitch from the wrong side of the hem edge (Fig. 3–14). Working from left to right, bring the needle up diagonally, catch a few threads of garment, and come up from the wrong side of the hem edge or seam binding. The needle should be angled down each time. This produces a series of slanting stitches.

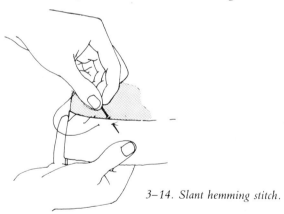

3–14. Slant hemming stitch.

Vertical Hemming Stitch This secures hems that are finished with woven edge or stretch-lace seam tape. This stitch is durable and stable and prevents fraying and breaking.

Work from left to right. Fasten the thread from the wrong side of the hem and bring needle and thread through the hem edge. Each stitch should be directly opposite this point and beside the hem edge. Direct the needle down, catching a few threads of the garment while going diagonally through the hem edge (Fig. 3–15). Stitches are ¼ inch apart.

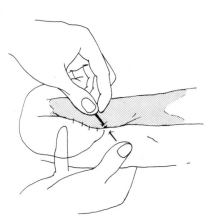

3–15. Vertical hemming stitch.

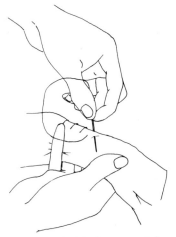

3–16. Overcast stitch.

OVERCAST STITCH

Use this to prevent a single thickness of fabric from raveling. The more the fabric will ravel, the closer together your stitches should be. In many cases, a row of machine stitching, ¼ inch from the rough edge, will serve as an anchor for the overcasting.

The stitches are diagonal over the edge. Secure the thread with a fastening stitch on the wrong side of the fabric. Hold the needle straight up and down, perpendicular to the fabric. Insert the needle on the wrong side of the fabric. The thread will go around the edge with each stitch (Fig. 3–16). Stitches are ¼ inch apart. Finish with a backstitch tack.

OVERHAND STITCH

Use this for holding two finished edges together, joining lace edgings, and securing the folded edge of a patch.

This stitch is similar to the overcast stitch, but the needle is inserted at a left–right diagonal. Secure the thread with a fastening stitch. Insert the needle at an angle from the back and through to the front (Fig. 3–17). Be careful to catch only a few threads at a time. Bring the thread directly behind the thread of the previous stitch and bring the needle out a stitch length away. Keep all the stitches the same size.

PICK STITCH

A decorative stitch on lapels, cuffs, pockets, and collars or an edge finish in tailoring, the pick stitch is used for topstitching and hand understitching when only the top part of the stitch should be seen.

The bottom layer of the fabric is not caught when taking the stitches. Tightness is not important here. This stitch should appear beadlike on the surface (Fig. 3–18). Remember, it is a decorative stitch. Proceed as you would for any of the backstitches, but remember not to catch the under layer of the fabric.

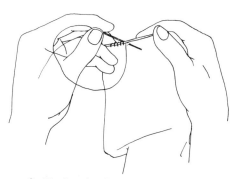

3–17. Overhand stitch.

3–18. Pick stitch.

PRICK STITCH

Use this for holding at least two pieces of fabric together, for sewing in a zipper by hand, and for preventing facings or linings from rolling to the outside of the garment. Actually, it is a variation of the backstitch, but more decorative. From the top you see only short stitches, but on the back side of the fabric you see long, overlapping stitches.

Catch the thread on the wrong side of the fabric. Be sure this is done securely. Working from left to right, insert the needle through all the fabric layers just behind your point of entry. Bring the needle ¼ inch beyond the point where the thread emerged originally. The stitches from the top will be very small (Fig. 3–19). Continue along your stitching line and finish off by pulling the thread to the under layer and securing it with a backstitch tack.

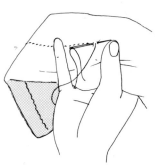

3–19. *Prick stitch.*

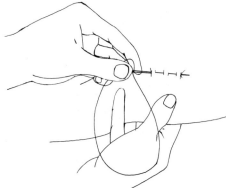

3–20. *Running stitch.*

RUNNING STITCH

The running stitch is different from the basting stitch in that it is shorter and permanent. It is used for gathering, preparing fabric for smocking, joining seams that have no strain, mending, and sewing trims.

Work from left to right and gather several small stitches on your needle before pulling thread through (Fig. 3–20). The stitches should be between ⅛ inch and ¼ inch long.

SADDLE STITCH

A decorative stitch on pockets, cuffs, collars, and edges, the saddle stitch is similar to the running stitch. The stitches are spaced further apart—approximately ½ inch and are done with buttonhole twist or embroidery floss—usually in a contrasting color.

Secure the thread on the wrong side with a fastening stitch. Work this stitch from the right side of the fabric. Starting on your left, weave the needle in and out of the fabric three or four times, space the stitches ½ inch apart (Fig. 3–21). Collect three or four stitches on the needle and pull the thread through—but not too tightly. Continue taking even stitches and end with a backstitch tack on the wrong side.

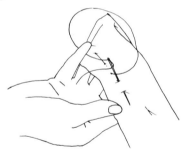

3–21. Saddle stitch.

SHELL STITCH

Used for finishing narrow hems and as a decorative edge for collars, cuffs, lingerie, and children's clothes, it is often called the "lingerie hemming stitch." By compressing the edge at intervals the stitch creates folds and gives a scalloped finish.

Start by marking every ½ inch with small dots along the length of the tucks between the scallops. Next, working from left to right, sew tiny running stitches between dots. At the designated intervals sew over each tuck, using two overhand stitches (Fig. 3–22). Keep the needle at a slight left-right angle. Always be sure to pull the thread taut before going to the next stitch.

SLIPSTITCHES

These stitches are almost invisible.

Uneven Slipstitch Actually, this is a flat hemming stitch used for bringing together a folded edge with a flat edge. It is also used for attaching trims and coat linings and is a good stitch for securing the edges of a facing to zipper tapes.

Work from left to right. Fasten thread with a knot and bring needle and thread out through folded edge. Remember to catch only one or two threads of the garment fabric and take very small stitches. In the folded edge, place the needle through the fold for a ¼-inch stitch (Fig. 3–23). Alternate the stitches from garment to fold.

Even Slipstitch Use this for attaching linings, pockets, and trim; for finishing hems; and for joining two folded edges together.

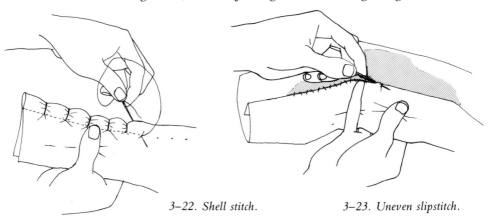

3–22. Shell stitch.   *3–23. Uneven slipstitch.*

Fasten the thread with a knot between the layers. Have the needle facing right and pick up one or two threads of the garment fabric very close to the edge of the folds (Fig. 3–24). Do this directly above your knot. Bring the needle through horizontally from the edge of the fold, ¼ inch to the right of the first stitch. Pull the threads through but not too tightly. Finish off with a backstitch tack.

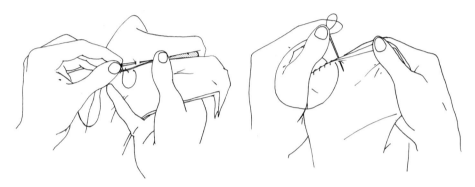

3–24. Even slipstitch.   *3–25. Whipstitch.*

WHIPSTITCH

The whipstitch holds two edges together. It is good for joining facings to a garment, for a fast hem, for attaching lace, tape, a hook and eye, and snaps. It is also for finishing waistbands and for appliqué.

The stitches will appear slanted because the needle is inserted at a right angle to the edge (Fig. 3–25). Secure the thread with a fastening stitch through the upper layer of the fabric. With one stitch, catch the fabric edges at the same time. Be careful to catch only one or two threads to prevent the stitch from showing on the right side of the fabric. Stitches should be evenly spaced. Finish by securing with a backstitch tack.

SPECIAL SEWING SITUATIONS

MANY GARMENTS will require hooks and eyes, snaps, hand-rolled hems, or darning. The following instructions should make all of these operations easy to do.

HOOKS AND EYES

Although hooks and eyes are small, they are very strong. They are used mainly at waistlines, cuffs, and neck edges. Sizes range from 0 to 3 (3 being the heaviest), and they are finished in nickel or black.

There are two types of eye available: the bar eye and the curved eye. The bar eye is used when the two pieces being joined will overlap (as in a waistband). The eye is placed on the right side of the lower layer; the hook is placed on the wrong side of the upper layer (Fig. 4–1A). Sew the hook on first, using a fastening stitch to secure thread. The hook should be ⅛ inch from the edge of the garment's upper layer. Using the whipstitch, pass the needle and thread

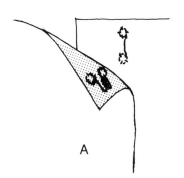 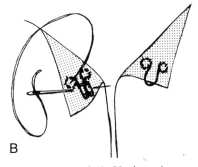

4–1. Hooks and eyes.

through the fabric around the circular holes. Don't forget to sew down the extension of the hook that will lie against the fabric (Fig. 4–1B). Sew a few stitches around the farthest flat part of the hook through one layer only. This will hold it securely in place but not show on outside of garment. Mark on the lower layer of the waistband or whatever, where the end of the hook will fall. The bar eye is whipstitched in place by passing the needle and thread through each hole, from left to right. Be sure to secure the thread.

The curved eye is used when the two pieces of fabric will butt one against another (as at a neckline). In this case both the hook and the eye are placed on the wrong side of the garment. The method of attaching them is the same as with the bar eye. However, the hook should be placed 1/16 inch from the edge, and the eye should be placed so as to extend slightly beyond the edge.

SNAPS

Snaps are small fasteners with less strength than hooks and eyes. They are used on overlapping edges where there is little strain. A snap consists of two parts: a ball and a socket. Snaps range in size from 4 (heavy-duty) to 0 (lightweight). Finishes range from nickel or black to clear nylon. The ball half is sewn on the wrong side of the upper layer, the socket half is sewn on the right side of the lower layer. (This is true for left-handers as well as right-handers.) Place the ball half on the wrong side of overlap, making sure it is far enough in from the edge not to show. In the ball half, whipstitch over each hold (Fig. 4–2A) and carry the thread under the snap when going from hole to hole (Fig. 4–2B). To mark the location of the socket half, rub tailor's chalk on the ball, position the closing, and apply pressure. Center the socket on the transferred mark. Start with the left hole and work from left to right.

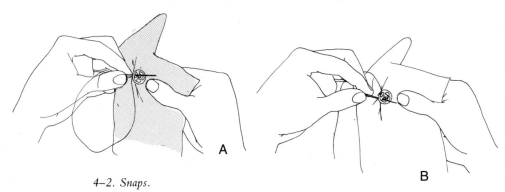

4–2. Snaps.

HAND-ROLLED HEMS

When a garment is made of a sheer fabric, as scarves and lingerie are, a hand-rolled hem gives a couturière finish. Although time-consuming, it is well worth the effort.

Using a close machine stitch, sew ¼ inch from the raw edge. Trim close to this line of stitching. Fold the hem to the wrong side just enough so that the stitching does not show. Work from left to right and take small stitches through the fold, then ⅛ inch below *and* beyond that stitch (Fig. 4–3A). Catch only a few threads of the garment. Pull the thread to roll the hem to the wrong side (Fig. 4–3B). Keep the stitches concealed as much as possible. Take only one stitch at a time, pulling thread only after six or seven stitches are taken. This does take practice. Secure with a backstitch tack.

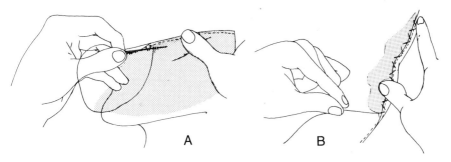

4–3. *Hand-rolled hem.*

DARNING

Darning replaces worn threads. Through the process of working stitches crosswise and lengthwise, a hole can be rewoven. Place the hole over a darning egg or, if you don't have one, a plastic container for lemon juice, a door knob, or a rubber ball.

Do the longer, lengthwise stitches first. Working from left to right, catch the raw edge enough to secure the thread, and bring the thread across to the opposite side. Work back and forth until the hole is covered. Then weave the crosswise stitches in and out of the lengthwise stitches (Fig. 4–4). Be sure these stitches are close together and do not pull at the edges; taut stitches lead to a puckered hole.

The suggested materials for darning are: three-strand embroidery floss, yarn, or cotton darning thread; a blunt or darning needle; and a darning egg or substitute. Be sure the color of thread matches the background as closely as possible.

4–4. *Darning.*

SEWING TRIMS BY HAND

SEWING BY MACHINE is always the preferred way, but there are some delicate trims that need special care and should be done by hand. Feathers, single sequins, rows of sequins, single beads, rows of beads, prestrung sequins, and sequin and bead combinations are attached in their own unique way.

FEATHERS

Finish the garment as directed. Make sure you have completed all the facings and have turned them to the inside and sewn them down. Wherever you are going to apply the feathers (armholes, sleeves, necklines, etc.), hand baste a row of stitches ½ inch from the edge. Using the row of basting stitches as a guideline, place the cord to which the feathers are attached on the right side of the garment. Pin over the cord to secure the feathers in place (Fig. 5–1A). At the end of the row of feathers, turn under the ends of the cord and whipstitch to the fabric (Fig. 5–1B). Be sure the feathers don't get caught in a zipper. If the end of the row of feathers comes around to meet the beginning, simply overlap the ends of the cord and whipstitch them together.

Turn the garment to the wrong side. On the wrong side, using thread that matches the feathers, sew a series of catch stitches every

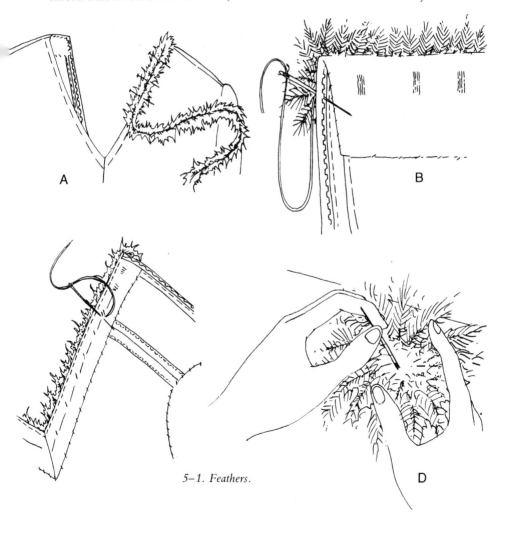

5–1. Feathers.

1½ inches over the basting stitch and the cord of the feathers (Fig. 5–1C). Because the feathers sometimes get caught in these catch stitches, turn the garments to the right side and fluff up the feathers, using a needle to pull the feathers apart (Fig. 5–1D).

SINGLE SEQUINS

Use a single strand of thread the color of the sequin and coat it with beeswax. Use tailor's chalk to mark the position of the sequin. On the chalk mark, make a few fastening stitches (Fig. 5–2A). With right side up, bring the needle up from the wrong side of the fabric. Run the needle through the hole in the sequin, making sure that the point comes up from the underside of the sequin. Slide the sequin down the thread to the fabric (Fig. 5–2B). Take a stitch on the left edge of the sequin down into the fabric and up again through the hole in the sequin (Fig. 5–2C). Insert the needle again at the right edge of the sequin. Pull the thread to the wrong side and fasten off. Be warned: applying single sequins is a time-consuming process.

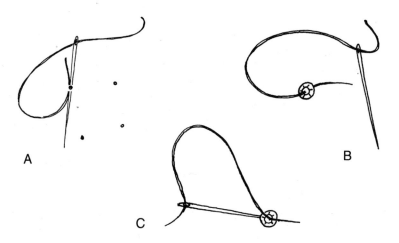

5–2. *Single sequins.*

ROWS OF SEQUINS

With a basting stitch, mark the placement for the sequins. *Never* use carbon paper and a tracing wheel for this. Apply the first sequin as you would a single sequin, but do not add fastening stitches. Bring the needle up through the right side of the fabric on the guideline, ⅛ inch from the edge of the first sequin (Fig. 5–3A). Slip the sequin, *wrong* side up, over the needle. Insert the needle through the fabric at the right hand edge of the first sequin, and bring it up again on the guideline, ¼-inch away (Fig. 5–3B). When you pull the thread

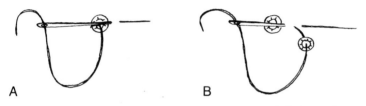

A   B

5–3. Row of sequins.

through, turn the second sequin over so the right side is up. Continue these steps until you have completed your row of sequins. To finish off, backstitch over the last stitch. Put the last sequin in place, and once again insert the needle at the right-hand edge of the sequin. Take some fastening stitches on the wrong side.

SINGLE BEADS

Mark the placement for the bead using tailor's chalk. Use a double strand of matching thread, coated with beeswax, and a slender needle. Take a few fastening stitches on the wrong side of the fabric. Bring the needle through the right side of the fabric at the position of the right-hand end of the bead. String the bead on the thread, and insert the needle to the left at the exact length of the bead (Fig. 5–4A). Pull the needle back up to the right side of the fabric at the right

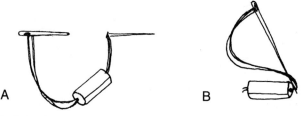

5–4. *Single bead.*

end of the bead. Do not pull the thread tightly. Once again, sew through the bead (Fig. 5–4B) and into the wrong side of the fabric. Fasten off on the wrong side.

ROWS OF BEADS

Using a basting stitch, *not* tailor's chalk, mark the placement for your row of beads. Start the first bead as you would when attaching a single bead. Going from left to right, place the needle at the point where the left-hand end of the first bead is to be located (Fig. 5–5A). Bring the needle out exactly one bead length away. String the second bead and insert the needle at the right-hand end. Bring it back up one bead length away (Fig. 5–5B). Continue adding beads until you have covered your row of basting stitches. Bring the last stitch up at the end of the last bead and back down in the same place. On the wrong side, fasten securely.

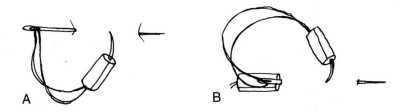

5–5. *Row of beads.*

PRESTRUNG SEQUINS

For every strip of sequins you apply, you will need an additional 12 inches of sequins for securing the band. Mark the placement lines using a basting stitch in a contrasting color. Remove 6 inches of sequins from one end of the strip. Place the resulting loose thread into a large-eyed needle. Insert the needle at the left-hand side of the placement line and pull out on the wrong side of the fabric. Tie off the ends. Thread a thin needle with a single strand of thread matching the sequin color. Secure on the wrong side and bring the thread up to the right side just between the first two sequins on the guideline (Fig. 5–6A). Insert the needle on the opposite side of the

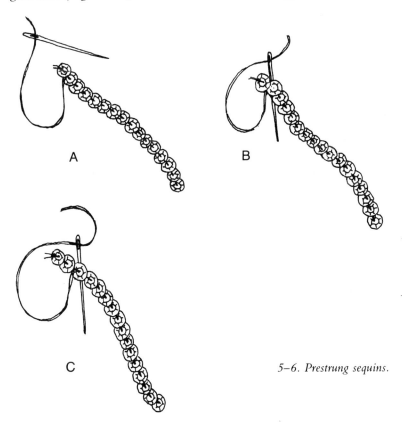

5–6. *Prestrung sequins.*

placement line (Fig. 5–6B). Do not pull the thread through, but repeat the stitch between the second and third sequins; then pull the thread through (Fig. 5–6C). Continue in this manner until the application is finished. Secure the thread on the wrong side. Strip the sequins off the last 6 inches of the band and repeat the process of pulling the thread through to the wrong side and knotting. Remove the original basting stitches.

SEQUIN AND BEAD COMBINATIONS

These are interesting because the sequins and beads are combined into one prestrung trim. The band of sequins will be the same length as the placement line. Loose beads and sequins must be secured at the

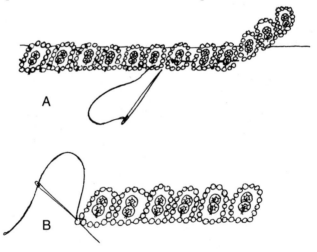

5–7. Sequins and beads.

edge of the band. With a slender needle and single strand of thread, sew down any loose threads on the wrong side of the band. With the fabric right side up and starting from the left side, baste the top of the band down to the fabric (Fig. 5–7A). Additionally secure the band in place with pins. Rethread the needle with a double strand of thread. Starting on the left side, bring the needle up from the wrong side to the right side. Make tiny stitches, catching the band, top and bottom (Fig. 5–7B), at sufficient intervals to hold it securely. At the end of the band, fasten off thread on the wrong side of the fabric.

TAILORING
HAND STITCHES

TAILORING IS SEWING SHAPE INTO MATERIAL. Tailoring requires hand stitches before pieces can be sewn together by machine. Once you have tackled these stitches you will see why tailoring is considered to be an art.

ARROWHEAD TACK

An arrowhead tack is an embroidery of two stitches slanted to form an arrow. It can be used singly or filled in as in satin stitch. Decorative as well as practical, it is often used as reinforcement at the top of a pleat. It is also used to reinforce pockets, seams, and buttonholes. In this triangular pattern, the stitches diminish on the parallel. This is done by working from two sides and gradually filling in the triangle.

Using tailor's chalk, mark the triangular arrowhead on the right side of the garment. Using a single thread, take two running stitches inside the lower right-hand corner of the triangle and bring the needle and thread out at that corner. At the upper corner, take a small stitch from left to right (Fig. 6–1A). Bring the thread through, insert the needle at the left-hand corner, and bring it out at the right corner (Fig. 6–1B). Bring the thread through. Continue working from left to right. The upper stitches get larger as they move down the sides of the triangle and the left-to-right stitches on the lower leg gradually become smaller. Continue until the triangle is completely filled (Figs. 6–1C and 6–D). Although this stitch isn't used every day, it is one that comes in handy, especially done the "left" way.

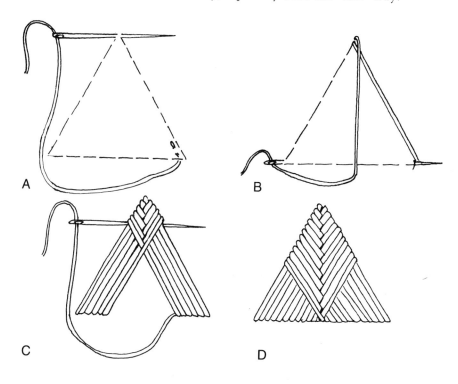

6–1. Arrowhead tack.

BAR TACK

Used for giving support to ends of seams, plackets, and slashes, the bar tack can be decorative on the right side of a garment (such as ends of pleats, buttonholes, and seams). It is also used at points of strain.

Use a double strand of thread. Knot the thread and bring to the right side of the fabric. Make a stitch the length of your tack. Repeat the stitch in the same place three times (Fig. 6–2A). Next, place the needle under the thread bar at the right-hand edge (Fig. 6–2B). Keep the needle over the loop of thread and pull through (Fig. 6–2C). Tighten this stitch as close to the edge as possible. Continue

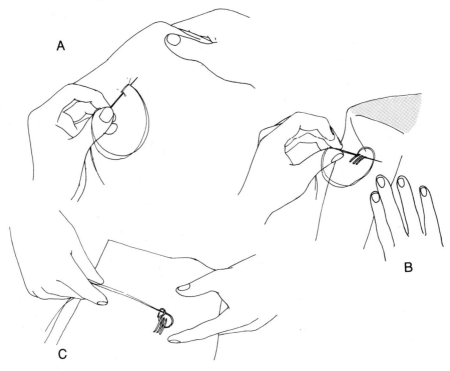

6–2. Bar tack.

across the thread bar, keeping the stitches as close to each other as possible. When you have completely covered the bar, insert the needle to the wrong side and secure with a backstitch tack.

BUTTONHOLE STITCH

Used for making hand-worked buttonholes, it can also be used for decorative purposes on the edge of your garment. Use buttonhole twist or a double strand of regular thread. Apply beeswax to the thread to prevent knotting.

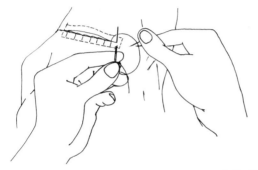

6–3. Buttonhole stitch.

Mark placement for buttonhole. Using a tiny machine stitch, sew completely around the buttonhole, ⅛ inch from the mark. Using buttonhole scissors, slash down the middle of your stitches. You will need a 20-inch length of thread. Secure the thread from the wrong side. Work from right to left. Stitches will go from the machine-stitched area to the slashed area. Insert the needle through the machine stitch and out through the hole. Be sure the thread is behind the needle (Fig. 6–3). Draw the thread through to form the knot on the buttonhole edge. Keep stitches close together and continue around the hole. Bar tack the edges by taking a few stitches across the width at each end of the buttonhole. End by bringing the needle to the wrong side and fasten off.

CHAINSTITCH

The chainstitch and the thread chain look alike, but they are used for different reasons. The chainstitch is used for reinforcing areas of stress. The loops are caught and secured onto the fabric.

Use a double strand of thread or a single strand of buttonhole twist. Secure the thread by using a knot and two small overlapping stitches. Work from left to right. Bring the needle to the right side of fabric. Your needle goes to the right, and the thread must be held to

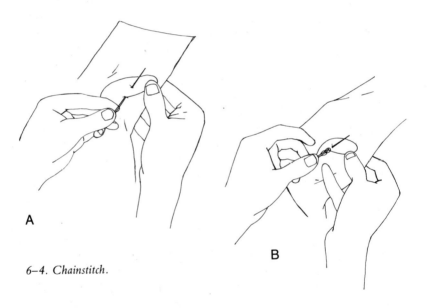

A

B

6–4. Chainstitch.

the right of the stitch, under the needle (Fig. 6–4A). Insert the needle just behind where the thread emerged. Be sure to insert the needle *inside* the previous chain and bring it out ¼ inch to the right (Fig. 6–4B). Continue to your desired length. End by inserting the needle down to the wrong side, *outside* the last loop. Secure with a backstitch tack.

THREAD CHAIN

A thread chain is separate from the fabric and is used for belt carriers and lingerie strap holders. It can be made as long as necessary.

Use a double strand of thread or a single strand of buttonhole twist. Secure with a knot on the wrong side and bring needle to the right side. Draw thread through and leave about a 5-inch loop. Use your right hand to hold this loop open (Fig. 6–5A). Hold the needle and thread with your left thumb and index finger. Reach through and grab the thread with the right hand and start a new loop (Fig. 6–5B). Repeat this procedure; new loops will form while the previous ones fall off and become smaller. This can be continued forever. To end, slip the needle through the last loop and fasten to the garment.

BLIND CATCH STITCH

This is the same as a catch stitch, but it is used for heavy fabrics between the hem and garment (like a blind hemstitch). It is more secure than a hemming stitch because of the crisscrossing.

This is one time you work from right to left. Place pins ¼ inch

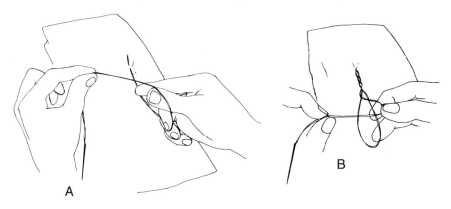

6–5. *Thread chains.*

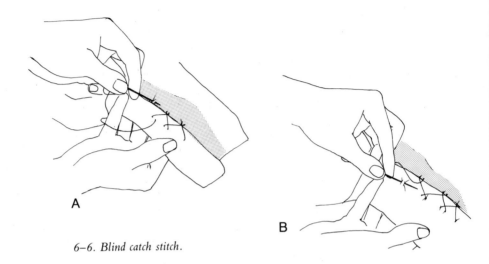

6–6. Blind catch stitch.

down from the hem edge. Secure thread with a fastening stitch on the wrong side of hem. Fold back the hem edge and; with the needle pointing to the right, take a small stitch on the right edge of the garment (Fig. 6–6A). Be sure your needle continues to face to the right, while the stitches move to the left. Alternate stitches from hem to garment (Fig. 6–6B). End with a backstitch tack.

CROSS STITCH

The cross stitch is a functional stitch that can also be decorative. It is used for holding folds in place, at the center back of jackets and coat linings, and as a single stitch to hold facings in place.

Secure the thread on the wrong side with a fastening stitch. Bring thread to the right side. Take a ½-inch, left-to-right stitch ½ inch above the fastening stitch (Fig. 6–7A). When pulled through, the thread will be diagonal. "Cross stitch," inserting the needle ½ inch to the left of the base of the original stitch (Fig. 6–7B), bringing it back to the right side, ½ inch to the right of the top of the original diagonal. Continue this pattern (Fig. 6–7C), keeping the stitches close together but not too tight. Secure at the end with a backstitch tack.

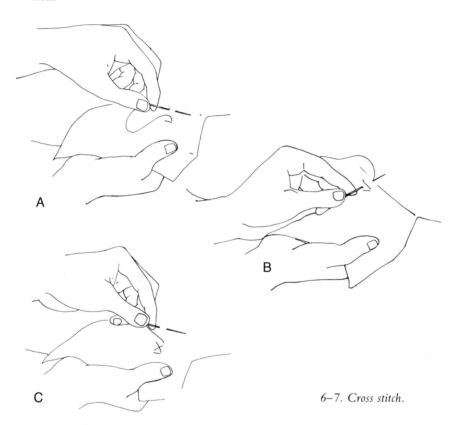

A

B

C

6–7. Cross stitch.

FELLING STITCH

Use this stitch for bringing a folded edge and a seam line together, as in linings on sleeves and at coat hems. Also use it for stitching down collars during the tailoring process, and for finishing the inside of waistbands, and for attaching tape to seam edges.

Insert the needle and secure on the wrong side. Bring the needle up through on the left side. The key is to sew horizontally at all times (Fig. 6–8). Take a piece of the fabric on each section, keeping your stitches ¼ to ½ inch apart.

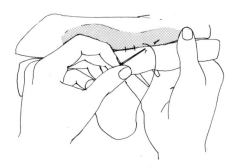

6–8. Felling stitch.

FRENCH TACK

Use a French tack for holding linings in place, for attaching belts to a garment—whenever there needs to be a distance between two surfaces.

Make a thread bar at the seam area between the lining and the garment edge (Fig. 6–9A). Go back and forth between the lining and the garment edge three times. Secure with one stitch on the right side of the thread bar. To make the chain section of the French tack, insert the needle through the loops of threads as you would in the buttonhole stitch (Fig. 6–9B). Cover the entire length of the thread bar.

PADDING STITCH

Used for attaching interfacing to undercollars, lapels, and front sections in the process of tailoring, the padding stitch will permanently attach at least two layers of fabric. It also holds interlinings in

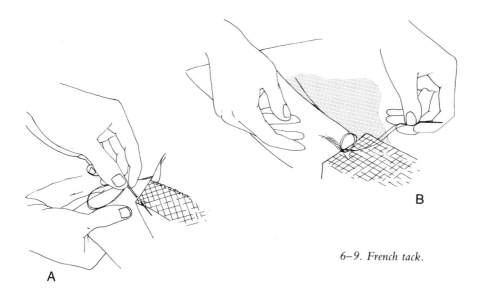

B

A

6–9. French tack.

place and secures the roll line. As you work up and down the roll line, you are sewing in the shape. These stitches remain, so catch only a thread of the outer fabric. Practice this stitch first on scraps.

This is one stitch that works better when done on your lap. Thread the needle with a knotted thread and begin by bringing out the needle between the interfacing and the upper layer of fabric at the lower left of the area to be padded. Bring the needle up and left ½ inch. Keep the thread to the left of the needle and take a horizontal stitch from left to right so that the needle emerges directly above the point where the thread first came out. Push the needle through. Bring the needle up and left the same distance as before and remember to keep the thread to the left of the needle (Fig. 6–10A). Take another horizontal stitch, from left to right, above the previous stitch. Continue to the top of the row. Insert the needle 1 inch to the right of the top of the last stitch and begin the next row (Fig. 6–10B). These stitches will slant in the opposite direction. Take

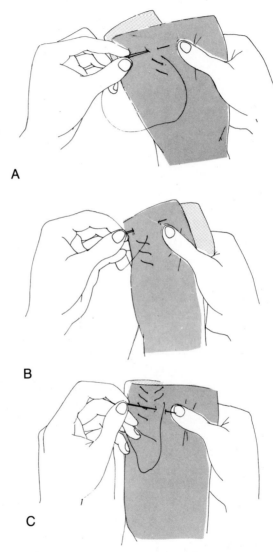

A

B

C

6–10. Padding stitch.

another stitch from left to right, this time beginning below and to the left of where the thread emerged (Fig. 6–10C). Now you will work from top to bottom. This method will give you the chevron padding stitch. Always secure with a backstitch tack and pick up where you left off as your thread runs out.

STAB STITCH

This is used for holding shoulder pads in place.

You must take one stitch at a time, because of the thickness involved. Use a single strand of thread and knot the end. Push the

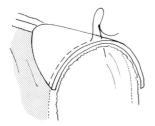

6–11. Stab stitch.

needle directly through all thicknesses of shoulder pad and armhole seam allowance (Fig. 6–11). Don't squeeze the pad by pulling hard, but make secure. You are actually doing basting stitches but only one at a time.

INDEX